Kid Power
HEALTHY LIFESTYLES FOR KIDS

Super snacks

Bobbie Kalman

Crabtree Publishing Company

www.crabtreebooks.com

Created by Bobbie Kalman

For Reverend Jane Drotar,
who fills me with awe!

Author and Publisher
Bobbie Kalman

Editorial director
Niki Walker

Editor
Kathryn Smithyman

Art director
Robert MacGregor

Design
Bobbie Kalman
Katherine Kantor
Samantha Crabtree

Production coordinator
Heather Fitzpatrick

Digital prepress
Embassy Graphics

Special thanks
Alexis Gaddishaw, Robin Turner, Sophie Izikson, Martin Izikson,
David Kanters, Andrew Key, Chantelle Styres, Jacquelyn Labonté, Erica Olarte,
Sara Paton, Jeremy Payne, Janelle Pyfrom, Catherine Pyfrom, Christina Pyfrom,
Jodi Pyfrom, Fruzan Langdon, Ian Bethell, and Adam Vok

Consultant
Valerie Martin, Registered Nutrition Consultant,
    International Organization of Nutrition Consultants

Food preparation
Valerie Martin

Photographs
All photographs by Bobbie Kalman except the following:
Marc Crabtree: back cover (right), pages 6 (middle), 30 (bottom left)
Other images by Comstock and PhotoDisc

Illustrations
All illustrations by Barbara Bedell, except the following:
Tiffany Wybouw: pages 28 (top and bottom left), 29

Printer
Worzalla Publishing

Crabtree Publishing Company
www.crabtreebooks.com   1-800-387-7650

PMB 16A	612 Welland Avenue	73 Lime Walk
350 Fifth Avenue	St. Catharines	Headington
Suite 3308	Ontario	Oxford
New York, NY	Canada	OX3 7AD
10118	L2M 5V6	United Kingdom

Cataloging-in-Publication Data
Kalman, Bobbie
 Super snacks / Bobbie Kalman.
    p. cm. -- (Kid power)
Includes index.
Explores why and how to have delicious and healthy snacks
through nutrition facts and easy recipes for nourishing foods.
  ISBN 0-7787-1252-4 (RLB) -- ISBN 0-7787-1274-5 (pbk.)
  1. Snack foods--Juvenile literature. [1. Snack foods. 2. Food habits.
3. Cookery.] I. Title. II. Series.
  TX740.K273 2003
  641.5'3--dc21
                                                        2003001794
                                                        LC

CONTENTS

SNACKING IS IMPORTANT!

Some nutritionists feel that eating five or six times a day—three meals and two to three snacks—is healthiest for our bodies. The snacks should be smaller than the main meals, however. When you eat frequently, but in small amounts, you get a steady supply of **energy** all day long. Energy is the power your body needs to function properly. **Nutritious** foods give you that energy. They contain the **nutrients**, or nourishing things, your body needs. If you do not feed your body enough nutritious foods, you will feel tired and weak. The recipes in this book are made from fresh ingredients. You'll be eating delicious foods that your body can use to make energy. Packaged snacks, which you may now be eating, are highly **processed**. Processed foods have been treated with chemicals that harm your body. Most packaged snacks also contain a lot of fat, salt, and sugar.

Healthy choices
- Drink plenty of water (see pages 6-7).
- Choose fresh fruits and vegetables as snacks.
- Read the labels on the packaging of processed snacks to learn what you are really eating. If you can't pronounce the ingredients in a packaged snack, don't eat that snack.
- If you crave sweets, stop eating foods that contain sugar and white flour, and your cravings for these foods will stop in a few days.
- Drink water, juice, or milk, instead of sodas or sweetened fruit drinks.
- Be physically active every day.

You'll love these snacks!
The children you see on these pages are not models—they are kids just like you. They made the snacks in this book and loved how they tasted! We know that you, too, will love them. Not only are these snacks delicious, but they will also make you feel good. Get your whole family involved in healthy snacking and healthy living, too. You'll soon see a big change in the way you all feel!

A bit about nutrients

Nutrients are substances in foods that your body needs to grow, heal, and function. The seven essential nutrients, listed in order of importance are: water, carbohydrates, fats, proteins, vitamins, minerals, and enzymes. Your body needs all seven to work at its best. Eating a variety of foods gives your body—and brain—maximum power.

Carbohydrates

Carbohydrates are your body's main source of energy. There are three kinds of carbohydrates—**simple**, **complex**, and **fiber**. Some are better for you than others. Simple carbohydrates are found in sugar and in white-flour products such as cake. They turn to fat quickly in your body. Simple carbohydrates are also found in fruits and in some vegetables, but these foods also contain fiber and other nutrients your body can use. Whole-grain foods such as whole-wheat bread and many vegetables contain complex carbohydrates. These foods release energy more slowly than simple carbohydrates do, so you feel energized for a longer time. Complex carbohydrates also contain fiber, which helps remove wastes from your body.

Proteins

Proteins are your body's building blocks. They are found in meat, fish and seafood, eggs, milk and soy products, and **legumes**, or dried beans. There are two types of proteins: **complete** and **incomplete**. Complete proteins are in meat, eggs, and milk products. Incomplete proteins are found in beans and grains. When you combine some incomplete proteins, you get a complete protein. Spreading hummus (see page 20) on whole-wheat pita bread, for example, turns these two foods into a complete protein.

Good fats and bad fats

You need fats to make new cells and to **absorb**, or take in, certain vitamins. Fats contained in olive oil, fish, and nuts are good for you, but the fats found in most processed foods stop your cells from growing normally. These fats harm your body.

Vitamins

Vitamins are in all fresh foods. Cooking destroys many vitamins, so it is important to eat some **raw**, or uncooked, vegetables and fruits each day. Vitamins such as A, C, D, E, and K are essential to your body. They are also important in maintaining a healthy **immune system**, which fights diseases and keeps you from getting sick. Your immune system also helps you heal when you are sick or injured.

Enzymes

Enzymes are found in all fresh vegetables and fruits, especially in **organic** foods. You need enzymes to break down the food you eat so your body can absorb the nutrients it needs.

Minerals

Minerals include calcium, iron, potassium, magnesium, and zinc. They are as important as vitamins. Calcium, for example, helps build your bones. It is found in milk, meat, almonds, and green vegetables.

5

WHY YOUR BODY NEEDS WATER

Water is the most important nutrient—you could not live without it for more than five days! 60 to 75 percent of your body is water. Your bones are 22 percent water, your muscles are 70 percent water, your blood is 83 percent water, and your brain is 75 percent water. Without water, your brain, muscles, bones, organs, and **metabolism** stop working! Your metabolism helps change the food you eat into energy.

Your body's water supply:

- controls your body temperature
- keeps your skin healthy and smooth
- develops your muscles
- helps **lubricate**, or moisten, your food so you can digest it
- lubricates your eyes, nose, mouth, and every joint in your body so you can move
- carries nutrients, energy, and information to and from your cells
- helps your body get rid of wastes

The dangers of dehydration

Dehydration means losing water from your body. Being dehydrated can be dangerous! When you are dehydrated, your temperature rises, and your body loses minerals such as sodium and potassium. It is especially dangerous in hot weather or when you're physically active. Most people are slightly dehydrated all the time and don't even know it. Drink water throughout the day—before you feel thirsty. If you are thirsty, you are already dehydrated!

The best drink by far!

Many people drink sodas when they are thirsty, but they are doing the opposite of what their bodies need. Sodas contain caffeine, which takes water out of your body instead of adding water to it. Each can of soda also contains phosphorous and nine teaspoons of sugar! Too much phosphorous and caffeine can rob your bones of calcium, so if you are drinking sodas every day, your bones may be getting thinner! Vegetable juices, teas, and fruit juices add water to your body, but some contain sugar or salt. The best way to keep your body hydrated is to drink plenty of pure water!

Dehydration warning signs

Do you know the warning signs of dehydration? You might be dehydrated if you…

- are extremely thirsty
- are extremely hungry
- feel light-headed or dizzy
- feel hot
- are unable to concentrate
- have a dry mouth
- feel extremely tired
- are unusually clumsy
- have muscle spasms
- have a headache
- are short of breath
- have a rapid pulse
- have blurred vision

Drink plenty of water

You should try to drink at least 6-8 glasses of water a day. This amount sounds like a lot, but these tips can help you drink the water you need.

- Drink one to two glasses of water as soon as you get up in the morning.
- Add a squirt of lemon juice to your first glass to get your digestive system going.
- Sip—don't gulp—a half glass of water every 30 minutes, even when you do not feel thirsty.
- Always drink water before and after exercise, but don't drink ice-cold water or cold liquids when your body is very hot.
- Drink plenty of water when you are working in front of a computer. Computers can dehydrate you quickly.
- To make water taste more delicious, flavor it with fresh fruit or vegetable slices, as shown on this page.

2 To make **Orange Water**, wash an orange and cut it in half with its rind on. Cut it again into quarters and then slice the quarters into thirds. Use half an orange to flavor a jug of water. Do not squeeze the orange juice into the water—just drop the pieces into the jug. Allow the water to stand for about 30 minutes. You can refill the jug once using the same orange pieces. Discard the orange pieces after about six hours.

1 To make **Strawberry Water**, wash and slice five or six strawberries and add the pieces to a bottle or pitcher of water. If you want to make only one glass, use one berry. Allow a half hour for the strawberries to flavor the water. Drink the water within six hours and then throw the berries away.

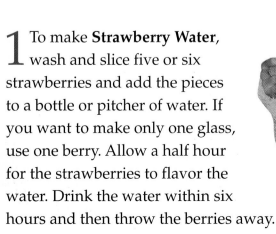

3 To make **Cucumber Water**, wash a cucumber and peel it if it is too waxy. If not, then leave on the peel and slice five or six pieces. Allow a half hour for the cucumber to flavor the water.

BE A CAUTIOUS COOK

Cooking is fun, but it can also be dangerous if you're not careful. When you are using the oven, stove, a knife, or a food processor, make sure there is an adult in the kitchen with you. Accidents such as burns and cuts can happen quickly! **Allergies** are another common food-related problem. Before you start cooking, have an adult who knows your allergies check over each recipe's ingredients. Some foods may contain ingredients such as nut oils. If you are allergic to nuts, be careful to read the labels on foods such as dried fruits and seeds. Nut oils can be found in many processed snacks.

More safety tips

•Before and after handling food, wash with detergent and water all the surfaces on which you are working, such as cutting boards and countertops.

•Then wash your hands. Always wash your hands with soap and warm water after handling eggs and raw meat. When washing up, include your palms, the backs of your hands, your fingertips and nails, and between your fingers. How long do you wash your hands? As you soap your hands, sing the Happy Birthday song. Do not stop soaping until you have finished the song. Then rinse with warm water.

•Be sure to wash any raw vegetables and fruits thoroughly before you cook or eat them.

•Always wear oven mitts when you handle anything in the oven.

•Turn the handles of pots and pans away from the edge of the stove so you do not accidentally knock them and spill hot food on yourself or others.

•If your hair is long, tie it back so that it does not touch the food or get in the way while you are cooking.

COOKING TERMS

When using the recipes in this book, you may see some cooking **terms**, or special words, that aren't familiar to you. The pictures shown here illustrate some of these terms. The recipes also include metric measurements in brackets. The letter "l" stands for liter, and the letters "ml" mean milliliter. When you see the words **teaspoon**, **tablespoon**, or **cup** without metric amounts beside them, you can use a regular cup, teaspoon, or tablespoon from your kitchen. In fact, many of the ingredients in this book do not have to be exact. We use terms such as **sprinkle**, **dash**, **drizzle**, **pinch**, and **handful**. When you see these words, you can use a bit more or less of an ingredient.

slice, chop: *cut food into even pieces*

dice: *cut food into small squares*

core: *remove stem and seeds from the center of fruit*

grease: *cover a pan with oil or butter so food won't stick*

drizzle: *pour a small amount of liquid slowly*

mince, press: *squeeze food such as garlic through a press*

purée: *blend food into a smooth paste*

grate: *rub ingredient against a grater*

blend: *put ingredients into a blender to mix them well*

mix, blend: *add ingredients while stirring*

handful: *an amount that fits in your hand*

sprinkle: *scatter solid or liquid particles over food*

9

SNACK PIZZAS

Pizza is fun to eat any time of the day! People like it because there are so many ways to make it. You can make large pizzas or small snack pizzas. To make a snack pizza, use a pocketless pita bread as your crust, as shown here. If you like veggies, make a pepper-and-onion pizza. If you like fruit, make an apple-raisin pizza or a Hawaiian pizza with pineapples and some strips of ham! Eat only half a pizza, though, so you leave some room for dinner!

To make a veggie pizza, you need:
- one pocketless pita bread (preferably whole grain)
- a handful of grated cheese (swiss, mozzarella, or cheddar)
- any of the following toppings: pepper rings, apple slices, canned or fresh pineapple chunks, chopped parsley, onions, raisins, dried cranberries, tomatoes, ham

1 Slice some pepper and onion rings and chop some parsley.

2 Use grated cheese or grate your own. Spread the cheese on the pita. Add the peppers, onions, and a handful of parsley. Read the baking instructions on the opposite page.

This pizza is beautiful and delicious!

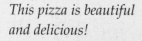

3 To make a Hawaiian pizza, sprinkle some cheese on the pita, lay down four strips of ham, and add the raisins and pineapples, as shown on the right and below. Put a sprig of parsley in the center of the pizza.

4 To make an apple-raisin-cheddar pizza, shown below, sprinkle cheese on the pita, cut some apple pieces, and arrange them in a circle. Sprinkle some raisins on the pizza and bake.

5 Preheat the oven to 400°F (200°C). Using oven mitts, put your pizza into the oven. Set the timer for ten minutes and check to see if the pizza is ready. When the cheese has melted, your pizza is done. Enjoy!

11

APPLE-CRANBERRY CRISP

This snack is is so yummy, it is like a dessert! It is also very nutritious because it contains a variety of foods—fresh fruits, dried fruits, grains, milk, nuts, and seeds. The "crisp" part of this snack is made with granola. You can use packaged granola, but our homemade version is so delicious, you will definitely prefer it! Use any leftover granola for breakfast or have it as a snack with some milk. To make a delicious dessert, add a scoop of vanilla ice cream to your Apple-Cranberry Crisp. This recipe makes 8-10 servings.

Fruit-bottom ingredients
- 4 large apples, peeled and cored
- ½ cup fresh or frozen cranberries
- 2 tablespoons liquid honey
- 1 cup granola (see recipe on the next page)
- 1 teaspoon cinnamon

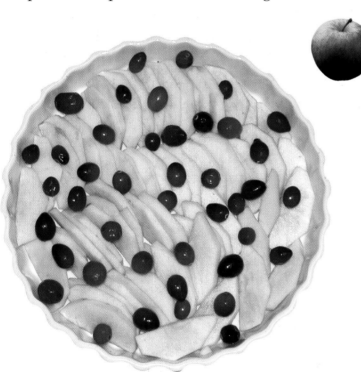

1 Slice the peeled and cored apples and place them on the bottom of a baking dish, as shown above.

2 Dot the apples with cranberries. Drizzle a little honey on the fruit and sprinkle it with cinnamon.

Granola topping

Dry ingredients:

- 3 cups (750 ml) oatmeal
- ½ cup (125 ml) sesame seeds
- ½ cup (125 ml) sunflower seeds
- ½ cup (125 ml) wheat germ
- ¾ cup (185 ml) shredded coconut
- ½ cup (125 ml) powdered milk
- 1 cup (250 ml) chopped nuts
  (walnuts, cashews, or pecans)

Wet ingredients:

- ¼ cup (62 ml) sunflower oil
- ½ cup (125 ml) applesauce
- ½ cup (125 ml) orange or apple juice
- ¼ cup (62 ml) honey or maple syrup
- 2 teaspoons (10 ml) vanilla
- ½ cup (125 ml) raisins, dried cranberries,
  or other dried fruit (add later)

3 In a bowl, mix together the dry granola ingredients. Blend the wet ingredients in another bowl. Add the dried fruit later.

4 Grease a baking pan lightly with oil or use parchment paper to line the pan, as shown. Spread the granola mixture onto the pan. Preheat the oven to 300°F (150°C). Bake for 30 minutes or until the granola starts turning brown. Ask an adult to stir the granola often for you and to check whether it is done.

5 Add the dried fruit to the baked granola and allow the mixture to cool. Spoon the granola over the apples and cranberries.

6 Bake the crisp in a pre-heated 350°F (180°C) oven for 30 to 40 minutes. Serve it warm or cold. It is especially delicious warm with a spoonful of vanilla yogurt or ice cream.

YOGURT YUMMIES

You'll love these two snacks! Not only are they delicious, but they also supply your body with nutrients. Yogurt is made from milk, so it contains calcium and protein, and the fruit and granola are full of vitamins and fiber. These snacks are easy and fun to prepare! To make them more healthy, choose a low-fat yogurt and fresh fruit or canned fruit in juice, not syrup. The first snack is called Peaches and Cream, and the second is Strawberry Surprise. Use the homemade granola recipe on page 13 and be amazed by the delicious taste sensations! Each recipe makes a single serving.

Peaches and Cream
- a single-sized container of plain yogurt
- 1 fresh or canned peach (in juice)
- about a tablespoon of lightly toasted sliced almonds

1 Wash and peel a fresh peach, cut it in half, and remove the pit. If you are using a canned peach, drain the peach first.

2 Put the peach into a food processor and purée it until it until it is smooth.

Swirl the peach around in the yogurt until you have an artistic pattern.

3 Put the yogurt into a bowl or dessert glass. Swirl in the peach purée, using a toothpick or the end of a fork or spoon, as shown. Sprinkle the almonds on top. Too good to be true!

Strawberry Surprise

- a single-sized container of plain yogurt
- 4 fresh or 6 frozen strawberries, thawed
- ¼ cup (62 ml) granola

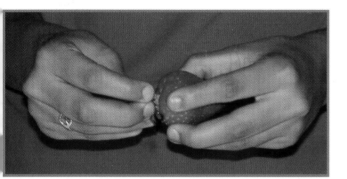

1 If you are using fresh strawberries, wash them well and pull off their leafy parts.

2 Cut the strawberries into bite-sized pieces and put them in a bowl.

3 Cover the bottom of a parfait glass with a layer of berries. Now add a layer of yogurt.

4 Sprinkle half of the granola over the yogurt. Repeat the layers by adding more fruit and yogurt. Top with the remaining granola.

15

ORANGE AMBROSIA

These identical sisters, known affectionately as the "Quads," live in Nassau, Bahamas, where it is always warm. All kinds of fruits grow in their garden year-round, such as oranges, bananas, mangos, papayas, lemons, and limes. No wonder their favorite snack, Orange Ambrosia, is made with fruit! Whether you get your oranges from a garden or a supermarket, they make delicious snacks because they taste great and contain many important nutrients. Orange Ambrosia is loaded with vitamin C and fiber.

To make one serving, you need:
- 1 orange
- 1 tablespoon (15 ml) concentrated orange juice
- about a tablespoon of shredded, unsweetened coconut

From left to right: Catherine, Christina, Jodi, and Janelle Pyfrom

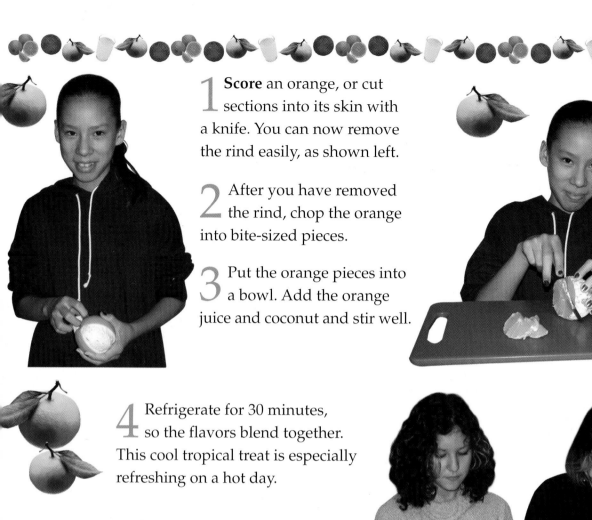

1 **Score** an orange, or cut sections into its skin with a knife. You can now remove the rind easily, as shown left.

2 After you have removed the rind, chop the orange into bite-sized pieces.

3 Put the orange pieces into a bowl. Add the orange juice and coconut and stir well.

4 Refrigerate for 30 minutes, so the flavors blend together. This cool tropical treat is especially refreshing on a hot day.

If you are sharing with a friend, simply double the recipe. How many oranges would you need to serve yourself and your sisters if you were one of the Quads?

TOMATOES ON TOAST

This wonderful recipe is a tasty and healthy after-school snack. It is very easy to make. All the ingredients are nutritious—and so delicious! Tomatoes contain vitamin C as well as many other important nutrients. Olive oil is a good fat that helps your heart. Garlic will keep colds away, and parsley and basil taste great! If you like garlic bread, you'll love Tomatoes on Toast.

For two servings you need:
- 2 small, ripe tomatoes
- 1 clove garlic, minced
- salt and freshly ground pepper
- 1 teaspoon (5 ml) olive oil
- a squirt of lemon
- a handful of fresh basil or parsley or both
- 2 pieces of whole-wheat or rye toast, cut in half

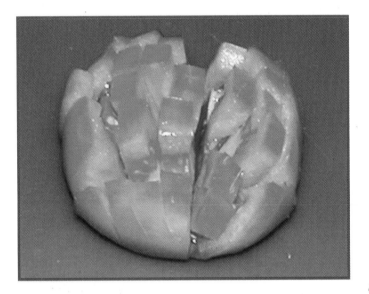

1 Wash the tomatoes and slice them crosswise, making a tomato bloom. When slicing, do not cut all the way down. Leave about a half inch (1 cm) uncut.

2 Turn the tomato on its side and slice it the other way, until you have small cubes, as shown. Discard the cores of the tomatoes.

3 Chop the parsley and slice some lemon and set them aside.

4 Mince the garlic by peeling it and squeezing it through a garlic press.

5 Put the tomatoes, garlic, parsley or basil, oil, salt and pepper, into a bowl or a jar. Squeeze a piece of lemon over the tomatoes and mix the ingredients well. Let the mixture stand for about 30 minutes to allow the flavors to blend.

6 While you are waiting, toast two pieces of bread and let them cool so they will be crispy.

7 Spoon the tomato mixture onto the toast and press it down so it will not fall off the bread. You can sprinkle a little grated cheese on top of the tomatoes, if you wish. Share your snack with a friend. There is plenty for two!

SPREADS FOR BREADS

The Quads are wondering what to spread on their crackers. We have two delicious recipes for them to try! One is called Heavenly Hummus, and the other is a cream-cheese spread that can be made in several flavors—and colors. All these spreads taste great on any kind of bread—pita wedges, toast, or crackers. Which spread do you think the Quads will like best? Try them all and guess which one the Quads chose.

To make 12 servings, you need
- 3 tablespoons (45 ml) lemon juice
- 1 tablespoon (15 ml) olive oil
- ¼ cup (62 ml) water
- 1 small garlic clove
- 1 teaspoon salt
- 1½ cups (375 ml) canned chick peas, drained
- 2 tablespoons (30 ml) tahini (optional)
- a handful of chopped parsley
- a dash of red pepper flakes

Heavenly Hummus
Hummus is a wonderful source of nutrients, including fiber. When you eat it with a grain such as pita or bread, it makes a complete protein. Besides being good for you, it tastes simply heavenly!

1 Drain the chick peas, put them in a colander, and rinse them under a tap until all the foam is gone. The foam in the beans causes digestive discomforts.

2 Blend all the ingredients, except the pepper flakes, in a food processor. Purée until the spread is smooth. Sprinkle on the pepper flakes. Use bread, crackers, or tiny pitas to scoop up the hummus.

Colorful cream-cheese spreads

This cream-cheese spread is mild, tasty, and a good source of protein. We call it Pink Spread because, when you blend in the red pepper, the cream cheese turns pink. To make Orange Spread, use a peach or orange instead of a pepper; for Yellow Spread, add about a half cup pineapple; for Green Spread, use half a green pepper or a stalk of celery; for Blue Spread, use about a half cup of blueberries. Which spread will you like best?

Pink Spread ingredients
- 1 roasted red pepper
- 1 cup (250 ml) low-fat cream cheese
- 1 teaspoon (5 ml) lemon juice
- salt and pepper to taste

1 Ask a parent to roast a red pepper for you or use a bottled roasted pepper. Remove any seeds.

2 Put the ingredients in a food processor and blend until the spread is smooth.

Which spread did the Quads choose? Although they look identical, each girl has her own tastes in food! Janelle likes the hummus, Catherine chose the Pink Spread, Christina liked the Green Spread, and Jodi loved the Blue Spread.

VEGGiES AND DiPS

Veggies and dips are a great snack and a healthy way to eat a variety of vegetables. Raw vegetables provide you with complex carbohydrates, vitamins, enzymes, and fiber. They help you control your appetite as well because they are crunchy, and it takes a long time to chew them. To keep this snack healthy, use only one or two tablespoons of dip. It takes very little to flavor the vegetables. The plate on the right shows some vegetables you can use for dipping. Cucumbers, zucchini, and broccoli are other good choices.

Zesty Dip
- ½ garlic clove, minced
- 1 finely grated orange or lemon zest
- 2 tablespoons (30 ml) orange juice
- ½ cup (125 ml) sour cream
- ½ cup (125 ml) plain yogurt
- 2 teaspoons (10 ml) chopped parsley or chives
- a sprinkle of pepper flakes

In a small bowl, blend the zest, juice, and minced garlic well. Stir in the yogurt. Cover the bowl and refrigerate for an hour or more. Add the parsley or chives just before serving. Sprinkle with pepper flakes if you like your food spicy! The picture above shows the right amount of dip to serve two people.

Cucumber Boats
- 1 small cucumber
- a sprinkle of salt
- freshly ground black pepper

The filling
- ½ cup (125 ml) low-fat cream cheese
- ¼ cup (62 ml) low-fat sour cream
- 1 spring onion, sliced
- ½ garlic clove
- ½ small red pepper
- ½ small green pepper
- 1 small carrot

Wash all the vegetables. Cut the cucumber in half lengthwise and scoop out the seeds, as shown above right. Sprinkle the "boats" with salt. Peel and chop the onion and peppers. Mince a peeled garlic clove. Peel and grate the carrot. Mix together the cream cheese, sour cream, onion, garlic, peppers, and carrot. Season with black pepper. Spoon the filling into the Cucumber Boats and cut the boats into five equal sections. Use only one-quarter of this dip for each boat. Refrigerate the rest of the filling for other after-school snacks.

1. To make a boat, scoop out the cucumber seeds with a spoon.

2. Squeeze the garlic through a garlic press.

3. Chop some red and green peppers into small pieces.

4. Grate the carrot.

5. Slice a spring onion.

6. Fill the cucumber boats with the dip and cut it into sections.

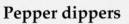

Pepper dippers
Instead of using a cucumber, cut a red or green pepper in half, scoop out the seeds, as shown, and use the pepper as a dip container. Fill it with the hummus (page 20), the cream-cheese spreads (page 21), or the Zesty Dip (page 22). Use your favorite veggies for dipping. When the veggies are gone, eat the pepper, which is now coated with the remaining dip. So yummy!

SiMPLY SUPER SUBS

Subs are delicious and nutritious, but don't eat a whole one! These sandwiches are a perfect snack to serve when a group of friends comes over after school. You can use just vegetables or add cheese and/or meat, depending on how hungry you are. To make your sub more healthy, choose low-fat cheeses and low-fat meats such as chicken and turkey. You can use one of the spreads on pages 20-23 and then add vegetables. Making a sub with a whole-wheat bun adds even more nutrients to your sandwich. Make your sub using the suggestions on these pages.

1 Before you make a sub, you need to have some "fixings" ready. Wash and dry some lettuce leaves and celery stalks and slice some peppers and tomatoes.

2 Choose your favorite kinds of cheese slices and put them on a plate.

3 Arrange your cold cuts on another platter. You can leave them flat or fold them in quarters so they will fit easily inside your sub.

4 You and your friends can now start creating your sub sandwiches to share. Start with lettuce, tomatoes, peppers, and add some cheese or meat, if you wish.

5 Cut your sub sandwich into at least four sections. For a snack, eat only one section with some celery or carrot sticks or cucumber slices. Wrap up the the rest, put it in the refrigerator, and take it to school for lunch the next day. Make sure you remove the tomatoes first, or you'll have a soggy sub!

BANANA ICE CREAM AND SHAKES

Bananas are naturally sweet, so they are a healthy alternative to chocolate bars, if your sweet-tooth happens to be acting up! You can use ripe fresh bananas to make delicious shakes or frozen bananas to make smoothies or some refreshing banana ice cream. If you feel tired, any of these snacks will give you a quick power boost.

Banana Milkshake

To make a banana milkshake, put a glass of low-fat milk into a blender. Add a banana, which has been broken into several pieces. Blend on high until the milkshake is frothy. This quick and refreshing snack makes one serving.

Banana Almond Shake

For one shake, pour a half glass of water into a bowl and add twelve whole **blanched** almonds. Pour the almonds and water into a blender and blend on HIGH, until the almonds are **pulverized**, or ground into powder, and the water looks like milk. Add a banana and blend again. This drink is a great dairy-free shake for those who cannot drink milk. It is rich in calcium and potassium.

You can buy blanched almonds or blanch your own. To blanch almonds, allow them to soak in hot water for an hour and then slide off their skins. The water releases the calcium in the almonds so your body can use this important mineral. The girl above is using more than twelve almonds because she is making several servings.

Banana Ice Cream

If your bananas are starting to get over-ripe, peel them and place them in the freezer in a plastic bag. When you want a really delicious treat, use one or two bananas to make the best ice cream you have ever eaten! Here is how you make it. Allow the bananas to thaw for about five minutes, or until you can break them easily. For each serving, use one and a half bananas. Put the bananas into a food processor and blend them until they start forming a paste. The frozen bananas will start to look just like ice cream—and taste just like ice cream as well! Eat your ice cream right away, or it will melt.

Keep several ripe bananas in the freezer to make delicious treats such as ice cream and smoothies.

The blended bananas look and taste just like ice cream. If your food processor has trouble blending the frozen bananas, add a few teaspoons of light cream or whole milk to moisten the bananas.

If you like chocolate, sprinkle a teaspoon or so of cocoa powder or baking-chocolate shavings on your ice cream. It will taste simply divine!

Strawberry Chocolate Kiss

2 frozen bananas
4 large strawberries
1 cup (250 ml) low-fat natural yogurt
1 cup (250 ml) milk or soy drink
2 or 3 teaspoons (10-15 ml) dark cocoa powder

Put all the ingredients into a blender and blend them until they are smooth. This recipe will make two super smoothies.

This smoothie recipe was created by Sophie, who is shown making it.

27

TRAIL MIX COOKIES

These cookies are made with oats, whole-wheat flour, seeds, and other delicious ingredients that will give you lasting energy. Eat one or two at recess or have one after school with a glass of milk, and you will feel satisfied until your next meal. The cookies contain complex carbohydrates, your best source of nutrition. This recipe makes about 24 small cookies. The cookies may be small in size, but they are huge in nutrition! We call them Trail Mix Cookies because trail mix contains nuts, seeds, and dried fruit, and it keeps you going for hours, just as these cookies do.

Dry Ingredients
- 2 cups (500 ml) quick-cooking oats
- 1½ cups (375 ml) soft whole-wheat pastry flour
- 2 teaspoons (30 ml) baking powder
- 3 teaspoons (45 ml) cinnamon
- 1 cup (250 ml) raisins
- ½ cup (125 ml) sunflower seeds
- ½ cup (125 ml) chopped walnuts

Wet Ingredients
- 1 cup (250 ml) sunflower oil
- ½ cup (125 ml) honey or maple syrup
- ¾ cup (185 ml) water

1 Preheat the oven to 350°F (180°C). Grease a cookie sheet lightly or use a non-stick baking sheet.

2 Mix the dry ingredients together in a large bowl.

3 Blend the wet ingredients in another bowl. Then add the wet ingredients to the dry ingredients to form a dough.

4 Form the cookie dough into small balls and put them on the cookie sheet. Flatten them with your hands or a fork to make patties. The dough should make between 24 and 30 cookies.

Don't forget to wear oven mitts when you put the cookies into the oven and when you take them out!

5 Bake the cookies in a preheated oven for 12-15 minutes. Allow them to cool.

6 You can take these cookies to school, on a walk with your dog, or enjoy them at home with a glass of milk. Dipping them in milk makes them taste great! Share the cookies with your family and friends, and you will be giving them a gift of energy.

AFTER SCHOOL FUN AND FOOD

Take your dog for a walk. You might have to carry it home!

After school is a great time to be active! You have been sitting at school for most of the day, and your body needs to MOVE! If you take part in sports, dance lessons, walk your dog, or ride your bike to and from school, you are probably getting the physical activity you need. If you go home and sit in front of a television set or a computer, you need to get more ACTIVE. Being active can be as easy as doing some stretches, running up and down the stairs a few times, or putting on your favorite tunes and dancing. Helping your parents with work around the house is another good way to move your body. Get active for at least 30 minutes each day.

Let your hair fly and...
Dance!
Dance!
Dance!

Find a book in the library that teaches you how to do ten basic stretches. Stretch your body often. You will feel great!

After you have been active for at least a half hour, have a snack and swing in a giant hammock with your sisters or friends. You've earned it!

Ten quick snacks

If you don't have time to make one of the wonderful snacks in this book, you can grab a simple snack that takes very little time to make or eat. Don't reach for a bag of potato chips or a box of cookies—have a nutritious quick snack instead. Here are some healthy ideas for those of you who are on the go.

1 Have some fruit. Fruit gives you instant energy and is filled with many nutrients such as vitamins, minerals, enzymes, and fiber. If you have time, make a fruit salad. It is so yummy!

2 Raw veggies taste delicious, even without dip! Carrots, celery, tomatoes, and broccoli are great for munching. If your mouth is tired, have glass of salt-free vegetable juice instead.

3 Tomato and low-fat cheese slices make a healthy snack. Add a piece of whole-wheat bread if you're very hungry.

4 A baked potato with sour cream and chives, yogurt, or shredded cheese is a wonderful treat. You can bake a potato in a microwave oven in 6-8 minutes. Then add the toppings.

5 A small bowl of homemade granola with low-fat milk will give you energy. (See page 13.)

6 Boil some eggs and put them in the refrigerator. When you need a snack, cut one in half and sprinkle it with hot sauce.

7 Cut a whole-wheat bagel in half and spread peanut butter on it. Add some apple or banana slices.

8 If you are not very hungry, just dip apple slices into peanut butter and skip the bagel.

9 Make your own flavored popcorn by sprinkling cinnamon, chili powder, cumin, pumpkin spice, or parmesan cheese on plain popcorn. A few drops of hot sauce makes popcorn spicy!

10 Dried fruits are as sweet as candy but are much better for you. You don't need to eat too much, though. Three or four dates, prunes, or apricots are plenty as a snack. These fruits are loaded with fiber and are so delicious! Nuts are another very healthy snack. Not only do nuts contain good fats that your body needs, but they keep you from feeling hungry for a long time. You can make your own trail mix by combining dried fruits with nuts and seeds.

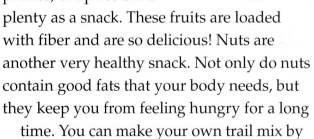

GLOSSARY

Note: Words that have been defined in the book may not appear in the glossary (Also see page 11 for cooking terms.)

allergy A negative reaction to certain foods

dehydration A dangerous lack of fluids in the body due to not drinking enough water or losing too much body fluid

digestive system A system of organs in the body that helps break down food

immune system A body system that fights disease and helps the body heal

legumes Dried beans

metabolic system (metabolism) A body system that changes nutrients into energy

organic Describing foods grown or prepared without the use of harmful pesticides

processed foods Foods to which sugar, color, or other chemicals have been added

score To make a shallow cut in a fruit or vegetable rind

whole grains Grains that have not been refined, or had their nutritous parts removed

INDEX

1 2 3 4 5 6 7 8 9 0 Printed in the U.S.A. 2 1 0 9 8 7 6 5 4 3